# 101 Ways to Save on Groceries

## Kristie Hammonds

# Inspire Publications

## A Division of

## Inspire Consultants

Copyright © 2011 Kristie Hammonds

For information about special discounts for bulk purchases, please contact sales@inspireconsultants.com

Inspire Consultants can bring this author to your live event. For more information or to book an event contact speakers@inspireconsultants.com

Cover Photo by Nathan Mantor Photography
Nathanmantorphotography.com

ISBN-10:061546825x
ISBN-13:978-0615468259

# DEDICATION

I dedicate this book to my wonderful family. Without their support and love I would not be where I am today. They have taught me that the most precious things in life are free and for that I am thankful.

# ACKNOWLEDGMENTS

I would like to say a special thank you to all of the people who have taught me these tips throughout the years. It is through your willingness to share that I have been able to learn so many wonderful ways to save money.

Thank you to my husband who has taught me that we all have a limited supply of time, but we can make our time here more precious by how we invest it.

# INTRODUCTION

*In this book you will find a list of over one hundred ideas on ways to save money at the grocery store. People often ask me to share some of my favorite money saving tips for grocery shopping with them. Even though time doesn't usually permit me to share a hundred of them at once, I share as many of these tips as I can.*

*At my workshops and other events, I have been asked and encouraged to put some of my favorite tips into a book so that it would be more convenient for people to use. Here are one hundred and one of my personal favorite tips on saving money on your groceries.*

*Pick and choose the ideas that work for you and start there. After years of coupon shopping I have implemented these little by little. Please don't think that you have to do all of these to be successful. Start where you are comfortable and add more ways to save as time goes by. Just by reading over these ideas you will start to do more and more to cut spending on your groceries and household items. This list is not complete, it is ever growing and changing, as is the grocery industry itself.*

*My wish is that this book somehow provides you with the ability to live a fuller life.*

*Remember, with the money you save you will be able to give more to your community, do more with your family, and have more fun!*

*My hope for you is that you will...Spend Less, Live More!*

# Tip #1
## \*\*\*\*\*\*\*\*\*\*\*

*Always, always, always, have a list and coupons ready when you walk in the door of the grocery store. Don't be lured off track by putting things into the cart that are not on your list.*

Remember that you have invested precious time and energy into making your list. It is the grocery store's job to place impulse items throughout the store, don't give in to their marketing tactics, stay focused and spend less!

# Tip #2
## \*\*\*\*\*\*\*\*\*\*\*

*Try to shop on off peak days. Shopping on a Monday, Tuesday, or Wednesday will guarantee you the best price, selection, and best markdown deals!!*

# Tip #3
**\*\*\*\*\*\*\*\*\*\*\***

*Stock up on household items you know you will use like deodorant, toothpaste, and shampoo.  When a store has a great sale on these items and you have a coupon for them, you can usually get these for almost nothing, buy six at a time and you will have enough to last until the next great sale comes along.*

# Tip #4
**\*\*\*\*\*\*\*\*\*\***

*Keep your pantry, refrigerator, and freezer organized just like your grocery store. The store is depending on you to be disorganized at home and pick up items on impulse which you probably already have in your cupboard.*

# Tip #5
## \*\*\*\*\*\*\*\*\*\*\*

*Train your eye to look away from the middle shelves; grocery stores put the priciest items at eye level. You can usually find much better deals on the bottom shelves.*

Again, don't fall for the marketing tactics that stores and merchandisers use. Think of it as your mission to get out of the store with spending as little as possible. Shopping on the top and bottom shelves will save you a lot of money. Stores are hoping that you will not bend over or stretch up to find those deals, but the shopper who does spends less.

# Tip #6
\*\*\*\*\*\*\*\*\*\*\*

*Avoid buying produce in bulk. The price per weight might be more to purchase only two stalks of celery, but if your family will not eat celery and you only need it for one recipe that week, it will cost less than buying a bunch and throwing it away.*

# Tip #7

**\*\*\*\*\*\*\*\*\*\*\***

*When you get a great deal on a main ingredient that your family loves, buy enough to make their favorite recipe four times. When you are cooking the meal that week, quadruple the batch and save the rest in dishes that can be frozen and go straight to the oven.*

This is a great way to have an easy meal ready on those busy days that you need a quick idea. The more meals you can have in your freezer the less likely you will be to pick up fast food or order pizza. Think of all the money you will be saving, but also think of how much healthier a home cooked meal is, your family will love you for it!

# Tip #8
## **********

*Go to the store when you have plenty of time and preferably as few people with you as possible. The grocery store loves to see you walk in with your kids or a spouse, they know that you will be caught in conversation and not notice how many impulse items you have in your cart.*

# Tip #9
**********

*Grow herbs and vegetables at home. You don't need a huge garden for this to work. Start with a few containers, one with tomatoes, one with onions, and small pots for herbs. Not only will you save money on fresh produce, but your family will love the taste of fresh herbs and veggies in their meals.*

# Tip #10
\*\*\*\*\*\*\*\*\*\*

*When possible, shop after 7 p.m. in the deli. You will find great deals and markdowns on roasted chicken, potato salad, and lunch meat. The deli has to close and you will benefit from their overcooking.*

# Tip #11
**\*\*\*\*\*\*\*\*\*\*\***

*Plan your meals for the entire week before you leave the house to go shopping.*

The more prepared you are, the less you will spend. The great thing about this is that it saves you a lot of time throughout the week as well!

# Tip #12
**\*\*\*\*\*\*\*\*\*\***

*Make a list for your groceries after you have planned for meals, you will know what you need instead of what you might want.*

# Tip #13
**\*\*\*\*\*\*\*\*\*\*\***

*Get a raincheck.......... The store knows that most people are in a hurry and will usually not ask for a raincheck if they run out of their hot deal that week, spend the time to get the raincheck so you never miss a deal!!*

*A store will usually issue a raincheck that is good for thirty days, plenty of time to locate even better coupons for that item to get it at an even better price.*

# Tip #14
**\*\*\*\*\*\*\*\*\*\***

*Learn to stack store and manufacturer's coupons to maximize savings.*

# Tip #15
\*\*\*\*\*\*\*\*\*\*\*

*Know your store's coupon policy like the back of your hand. Sometimes store employees have not learned all there is to know about the coupon policy. Be proactive so that you will not be confused at the checkout.*

# Tip #16
**\*\*\*\*\*\*\*\*\*\***

## *Avoid the center of the aisle displays and the end caps.*

This is another one of those marketing tactics the store will use to make you impulse buy. They put very appealing displays where you will need to maneuver around them in the aisle and on the end of the aisle so that as you are turning the corner you will stop and look at the "great" sales. Beware; these are usually not good sales, rather part of their marketing plan.

# Tip #17
**\*\*\*\*\*\*\*\*\*\***

*Realize that a grocery store is open to make money; they want you to be hungry, your attention to be pulled in a million different directions, and to be able to reach for the most expensive items easily.*

# Tip #18
**\*\*\*\*\*\*\*\*\*\***

*Ask the store manager what time of the day, week, or month they mark down items to clearance price. Shop at that time before hundreds of people have had time to pick through them.*

# Tip #19
**\*\*\*\*\*\*\*\*\*\*\***

*When you pass a blinkie (little red coupon dispenser) grab two or three of those coupons. The price is usually not at rock bottom when they have the machine up, but if you save those coupons a sale will happen and you will be prepared.*

# Tip #20
## \*\*\*\*\*\*\*\*\*\*

*Try a different store,
Sometimes a new view can
save you a lot of money.*

# Tip #21
**\*\*\*\*\*\*\*\*\*\*\***

*Watch buying in bulk, make sure that if you are buying a large item that the price per ounce is less than a smaller package, and make sure your family loves it.*

# Tip #22
### \*\*\*\*\*\*\*\*\*\*\*

*Shop BOGO deals, most stores only require you to buy one of the items at half price, again know your stores policy so you can save more!*

*\*BOGO stands for Buy One Get One Free*

# Tip #23
\*\*\*\*\*\*\*\*\*\*\*

*Once a week plan a meatless meal. Meat is sometimes the most expensive part of a meal. Try veggie pizza, spaghetti with no meat sauce, or cheese and bean quesadillas.*

# Tip #24
\*\*\*\*\*\*\*\*\*\*\*

*Use canned chicken, buy it on sale with a coupon and a once expensive meal is now reduced by 75%.*

# Tip #25
**\*\*\*\*\*\*\*\*\*\*\***

*Sometimes buying normal grocery items are actually cheaper at a drugstore, always check their weekly sales, you can save on at least a few items each week.*

# Tip #26
# **********

*Don't feel guilty about using coupons, some people think that coupons cost the store money, they don't! The manufacturer sends the money on the coupon back to the grocery store.*

# Tip #27
**\*\*\*\*\*\*\*\*\*\*\***

*Coupons come off of a company's advertising budget; this is true for store coupons as well.*

# Tip #28
**\*\*\*\*\*\*\*\*\*\***

*Buy snacks for school lunches in large sizes and use store brand zipper bags to make them snack size.*

# Tip #29
\*\*\*\*\*\*\*\*\*\*\*

*Always look for tear pads of coupons, store coupon books, and any mail in rebate forms as you shop. Take one or two and save them until you need them.*

# Tip #30
### \*\*\*\*\*\*\*\*\*\*\*

*Buy meat in "family size" packs and break into portion size as soon as you are home from the store. Put them in freezer bags and have a permanent marker to put the date it was frozen and the type of meat it is.*

Wrap the meat in wax paper or butcher paper before you put it in the bags. Always remember to write the cut of meat on the outside of the freezer bag with a permanent marker or you may be surprised when you defrost it for your meal!

# Tip #31
**\*\*\*\*\*\*\*\*\*\*\***

*Think of grocery shopping like a job, you get paid by the hour.  Spend one hour preparing your list and getting your coupons ready and one hour shopping, if you save $100 at the store, then you just made $50 an hour at your job........not bad pay in tough economic times.*

# Tip #32
## \*\*\*\*\*\*\*\*\*\*\*

*Be leery of marked down meat, a lot of the time the cut of meat that is on sale that week is actually less expensive than anything they have marked down.*

This is not always true, sometimes the "managers special", which is code for about to run out of date, is a great deal, just always check to make sure. Just because it is about to expire, if they have only marked it down 20% it is not a great deal. You would most likely be able to get it cheaper on sale.

# Tip #33
**************

*Don't fall into the stores marketing plan of spending $100 to save 10 cents a gallon on gas. If you have a 15 gallon gas tank you are only saving $1.50 per tank. You might be able to save more money by shopping at a different store.*

# Tip #34
\*\*\*\*\*\*\*\*\*\*

*Plan meals using the same main ingredients but have a different ending effect. Potatoes are a great example; you can slice them, bake them, and mash them. One food offers many options for your recipes.*

# Tip #35
**\*\*\*\*\*\*\*\*\*\*\***

*Don't cut all your coupons, just put them into file folders with the date and pull out the ones you need when you need them.*

This is for all the people out there who say "I don't have time to coupon shop." Sure you do, if you do it the right way it will be the best use of time for your family! Just find the way that is easiest and most convenient for you.

# Tip #36
**\*\*\*\*\*\*\*\*\*\***

*If you can get an item for free,
get it and find a recipe for it.
If you won't use it, donate it to
your church pantry, or local
shelter. Someone will love to
have your extras.*

# Tip #37
**\*\*\*\*\*\*\*\*\*\*\***

## *Use the store ad from a competitor and get a better price at your store.*

This tip is for the experienced coupon shopper who is ready to step to the next level. Caution: Don't do this on every item you buy, only for one or two items every week, don't be the person all the cashiers hide from when they see you walk into the store.

# Tip #38
**\*\*\*\*\*\*\*\*\*\***

*Know that a 10 for $10 sale does not mean you need to buy 10 of any one item or even 10 items combined, it just means that all the items on sale will ring up for $1.00 each.*

# Tip #39
**\*\*\*\*\*\*\*\*\*\*\***

*Have a price list either at home or one that you carry with you that lists all the rock bottom prices of the things you buy. That way when an item is on sale, you will know if it really is a great deal.*

# Tip #40
**\*\*\*\*\*\*\*\*\*\***

*Never feel like you need to use coupons just to use coupons, if you are using them effectively, there will be many that you won't use every month.*

# Tip #41
**\*\*\*\*\*\*\*\*\*\*\***

*Keep a folder with your grocery receipts for the past few months. If you start to feel like preparing for your trip isn't worth it, pull out that folder and you will get motivated again....fast!*

# Tip #42
**\*\*\*\*\*\*\*\*\*\***

*Have no brand loyalty. If you can get something for less money without giving up on quality, get it.*

# Tip #43
**********

*Plan your menus after you write down the sale prices for the meat and produce that week, you will build your menu around those items and save more than 50% on your grocery bill.*

# Tip #44
**\*\*\*\*\*\*\*\*\*\***

*If you can, use cash out of an envelope with your monthly "allowance" for groceries. Paying with cash gives you the ability to visually see how you are using your money.*

# Tip #45
**\*\*\*\*\*\*\*\*\*\*\***

*Print your own money at home...........printable coupons are the way to go. If you don't have one from your insert, print it from the manufacturer's website.*

# Tip #46
**\*\*\*\*\*\*\*\*\*\***

## *Ask friends or neighbors to give you their coupon inserts if they do not use them.*

You will be shocked at how many people do not use coupons, they love helping you by giving you the inserts though!

# Tip #47
**********

*Keep a running list of items
you need somewhere in your
kitchen, add items to the list as
you use them so that you
never run out.*

# Tip #48
**\*\*\*\*\*\*\*\*\*\***

*Make larger grocery trips. The fewer times you walk into the store the less you will be tempted to spend money.*

# Tip #49
**\*\*\*\*\*\*\*\*\*\*\***

*Write your list by store layout,
the less you wander the aisles,
the less temptation there will be
for impulse items.*

# Tip #50
**\*\*\*\*\*\*\*\*\*\*\***

*Try to shop at a store that doubles coupons. If you don't have a store that doubles, visit their website and suggest changing their coupon policy to include doubling, and while you are on the website, print any coupons they have available.*

# Tip #51
\*\*\*\*\*\*\*\*\*\*\*

*Learn your store's sale cycle and stock up on items according to how much your family will use before it goes on sale again.*

Every store has a sale cycle, but remember most items go on sale every three months, so buy enough of that item to last until it goes on sale again.

# Tip #52
**\*\*\*\*\*\*\*\*\*\***

*If at all possible, buy a chest freezer. Use the money you save for the first month using coupons to purchase one of these and save even more!*

# Tip #53
**********

*Avoid frozen prepared entrees, someone pays for the convenience of those items and it isn't the manufacturer.*

# Tip #54
**\*\*\*\*\*\*\*\*\*\*\***

*Drink more water, even bottled water is less expensive than sodas or juice.  Water is very healthy and we all need more of it!*

# Tip #55
**\*\*\*\*\*\*\*\*\*\*\***

*If you can't plant vegetables, visit the local farmers market. You can usually get produce at least a third off the grocery store prices.*

# Tip #56
**\*\*\*\*\*\*\*\*\*\***

*Freeze leftovers in the divided plates that you can get at the dollar store. This way you have lunch or a quick dinner and it doesn't cost any money!*

# Tip #57
**********

*Before you check out, look through your cart one quick time to put back a couple of items you bought on impulse.  Even the most well planned shopper can give into temptation occasionally, sometimes without even realizing it!*

# Tip #58
**\*\*\*\*\*\*\*\*\*\***

*Two times a month, eat completely from your pantry and freezer. This saves planning two meals and will use up any excess you might have.*

# Tip #59
**\*\*\*\*\*\*\*\*\*\*\***

*Try to find a quick and easy cookbook. My favorite is a four ingredient cookbook, obviously, the fewer ingredients, the easier it is!*

# Tip #60
\*\*\*\*\*\*\*\*\*\*\*

*Try to buy frozen fruits and vegetables when they are on sale. They are much cheaper than canned and are still very nutritious.*

# Tip #61
**\*\*\*\*\*\*\*\*\*\***

*Never run out of staple items like ketchup, mustard, salad dressing, and pickles. These items cost way too much to get if they are not on sale and you don't have a coupon. Always plan ahead and keep your staples stocked!*

# Tip #62
**\*\*\*\*\*\*\*\*\*\***

*Buy your meat from local farmers. Go to www.localharvest.com for some great deals in your area. The meat is usually a higher quality and much more affordable.*

# Tip #63
\*\*\*\*\*\*\*\*\*\*\*

*Buy frozen bread dough for bread, pizza crusts, rolls, and garlic bread. It is much less expensive than the prepackaged refrigerated dough.*

# Tip #64
**\*\*\*\*\*\*\*\*\*\***

*If your store has a loyalty card...use it. Go online to the store website and add coupons to your store card, these come off automatically at time of checkout and can make a big difference in your ending total.*

# Tip #65
**\*\*\*\*\*\*\*\*\*\*\***

*Always have a budget in mind and as you put items in your cart keep a running total in your head. If you reach your budgeted amount then you are done shopping.*

Keep a calculator with you for this, that way you don't have to think about a total the entire time you shop.

# Tip #66
**\*\*\*\*\*\*\*\*\*\***

*Don't "crisis cook", have
everything planned so that you
don't have to run to the store
every day after work.*

# Tip #67
\*\*\*\*\*\*\*\*\*\*\*

*Don't shop when you are tired. You will buy more sweets and carbohydrates.*

*Also, if you go when you are angry, you will buy more crunchy food which can be high in fat and calories and very high in price.*

# Tip #68
**\*\*\*\*\*\*\*\*\*\***

*Only buy mark downs if they save you at least 25% off the original price, any less than that and you are not saving as much as you could on a regular sale.*

# Tip #69
\*\*\*\*\*\*\*\*\*\*\*

*Talk to your newspaper delivery person. If they just throw away papers at the end of the day, see if you could work out a deal for him to give you the inserts out of them. Even with giving him a tip it is cheaper than buying that many papers.*

# Tip #70
**\*\*\*\*\*\*\*\*\*\***

*Don't overlook finding coupons in your favorite magazines. Your monthly subscription could not only be entertaining but can save you money at the grocery store.*

# Tip #71
**\*\*\*\*\*\*\*\*\*\***

*Usually try to avoid buying aspirin, contact lens solution, and vitamins at the grocery store. These items are typically less expensive at your drug store.*

# Tip #72
## \*\*\*\*\*\*\*\*\*\*

*Have an envelope where you put the money you save. If you can visually see your work is adding up, you will work even harder to save more.*

# Tip #73
**\*\*\*\*\*\*\*\*\*\*\***

*Don't throw away food.  A study has said that Americans throw away 14% of the food they buy. Shop only after you have planned a menu for the week.  If you have leftovers that means lunch is already "packed" for the next day!*

# Tip #74
\*\*\*\*\*\*\*\*\*\*\*

*Line the bottom of your crisper drawer with paper towels. This absorbs the moisture that causes your fresh veggies to go bad.*

# Tip #75
**********

*Keep your brown sugar in the freezer to keep it from hardening. If you already have hard brown sugar, place a slice of bread in a bag with the sugar, it will soften up very quickly.*

# Tip #76
\*\*\*\*\*\*\*\*\*\*

*The healthiest foods in the store are around the outside edges. That is where the dairy, meat, and produce sections are. Anything toward the middle is usually highly processed and costs more.*

# Tip #77
**************

*Brew your own cup of coffee, by skipping the store or gas station coffee you can save $800 a year!*

# Tip #78
**\*\*\*\*\*\*\*\*\*\***

*Plan one trip a month for big ticket items. This is when you would buy your toilet paper, paper towels, trash bags, laundry detergent, and any other household items you need. Buy them at a low price and with coupons and you will be surprised at how much lower your regular grocery bill will be!*

# Tip #79
**\*\*\*\*\*\*\*\*\*\***

*To keep herbs fresh, freeze them in freezer bags. When you are ready to use them you only need to chop off the appropriate amount and they will be in perfect shape as soon as they hit a hot pan.*

# Tip #80
**\*\*\*\*\*\*\*\*\*\*\***

*One night a week make plans for a slow cooker meal night. Recipes cooked in a slow cooker are usually less expensive, more flavorful, and take a lot less time to prepare than other recipes you may use.*

# Tip #81
************

*Watch the register, the sale prices do not always ring up at the time of checkout. Also, watch your fresh produce; sometimes new cashiers may not know the different codes for certain produce, so watch carefully.*

# Tip #82
**\*\*\*\*\*\*\*\*\*\***

*Weigh before you put produce in your cart. If you are buying a ten pound bag of potatoes, weigh them and get the most bang for your buck!*

# Tip #83
**********

*Buy cold cuts in the deli. The deli always has at least one cut of meat that is on sale for a great price, you will pay less and you don't have all the packaging to throw away.*

# Tip #84
**\*\*\*\*\*\*\*\*\*\***

*Shop the day after major holidays. After Thanksgiving, turkeys are almost free. Get a couple and put them in the freezer.*

# Tip #85
## \*\*\*\*\*\*\*\*\*\*\*

*Free samples can be requested and your mailbox will become your new best friend. You can try new items for free and save that money for something else.*

These items almost always come with great coupons! That way when the item goes on sale at the store, if you liked the sample you can get the full size for a great price.

# Tip #86
***********

*Think of coupons as cash and you may be more motivated to use them. It can be work to clip and organize coupons, but if you think of them as "found or free money", you may have a different attitude towards investing time collecting them.*

# Tip #87
************

*Trade your extra coupons.*

Forming a coupon swap group is great for everyone. We all have different wants when it comes to grocery items so it makes sense that if there is a group of people working together everyone wins. It is also a great way to have some fun with friends!

# Tip #88
**\*\*\*\*\*\*\*\*\*\***

*Sign up for all of the freebies you can. Not only do you get free stuff, but this puts you on mailing lists for future promotions, too.*

# Tip #89
**\*\*\*\*\*\*\*\*\*\***

*Realize that manufacturer's have cycles just like the stores, the coupons they place in Sunday papers are in there to get you to go to the store to buy those items right away. If you wait 2-3 weeks many of these items will be on sale and you can actually get lower prices.*

# Tip #90
## \*\*\*\*\*\*\*\*\*\*

*Make a commitment to only eat out a few times per month...or not at all.*

This shows your family what a special time it is to go out to eat. I remember when I was a little girl, we would only go out for very special occasions and it was so much fun. In America today, we are in such a hurry, it seems we are eating out all the time and having dinner at home is a special occasion.

# Tip #91
**\*\*\*\*\*\*\*\*\*\*\***

*Buy only what you will use; purchasing large amounts at a great price is wonderful, only if it doesn't go to waste.*

# Tip #92
**\*\*\*\*\*\*\*\*\*\*\***

*Contact manufacturers to ask for coupons and to compliment them on a great product. Everyone likes a compliment.*

# Tip #93
**\*\*\*\*\*\*\*\*\*\*\***

*Use your coupons on the smallest size product allowed. Typically these products cost less so you may get some items for free or close to free this way.*

# Tip #94
**\*\*\*\*\*\*\*\*\*\***

*Get together with your coupon swap club and start a pantry at your church with all the free items you were able to acquire in one month, think of how many people you can bless!*

# Tip #95
**\*\*\*\*\*\*\*\*\*\*\***

*Don't use a coupon for an item that you don't need or use unless you plan on donating it.*

# Tip #96
**\*\*\*\*\*\*\*\*\*\***

*Compare the price of large and medium eggs. If the large eggs are more than .07 cents higher than the medium eggs, medium eggs are the better buy.*

# Tip #97
**\*\*\*\*\*\*\*\*\*\***

*Learn to make soup; it is such a healthy and inexpensive meal.*

# Tip #98
**\*\*\*\*\*\*\*\*\*\***

*Find a pick your own farm and pick your own produce. This is great fun for the whole family and a lot cheaper than buying in season produce at the store. Also, you are helping a local farmer and their family and you know where it came from!*

# Tip #99
**********

*Bake at home: Prepackaged baked goods or fresh bakery items are more expensive.*

# Tip #100
**\*\*\*\*\*\*\*\*\*\***

*Make it your goal each time you are at the grocery to shave off just an extra 8.3%, which is 1/12[h]. That means that if you do this consistently, you will have saved enough for a month's free groceries at the end of the year!*

# Tip #101
\*\*\*\*\*\*\*\*\*\*\*

## If you feel like giving up...
## DON'T!

# Final Thoughts
**\*\*\*\*\*\*\*\*\*\*\*\*\*\*\*\***

*I hope you have enjoyed learning different ways that you can save on groceries and household items. As you can see, it is more than just saving money. A lot of the ideas in this book show you ways to spend more time with family, eat a healthier diet, and help local farmers and others in the community. The end result is that you are able to spend less and live more. After all, that is what this life is all about!*

*For additional money saving ideas,
extended learning products and to access
Kristie's national coupon data base visit,*

*www.couponshoppingforlife.com*

# ABOUT THE AUTHOR

Kristie lives in Nashville, Tennessee with her husband and three children. She is a former school teacher and a successful business woman. She has earned many awards and honors from Fortune 500 companies whom she has worked for. Today Kristie focuses her attention on helping families save money. Her website www.*couponshoppingforlife.com* provides up to date money saving tips and additional learning programs.

Kristie's unique approach to saving money combined with her ability to captivate an audience has made her a sought after speaker. She conducts seminars and workshops around the country sharing her inspiring message of *"Spend Less, Live More."*

To learn more about Kristie visit her at
*www. kristiehammonds.com*